EXPLORING SPACE™

Black Holes

Amanda Davis

The Rosen Publishing Group's
PowerKids Press™
New York

Published in 1997 by The Rosen Publishing Group, Inc.
29 East 21st Street, New York, NY 10010

First Edition

Book Design: Erin McKenna

Photo Credits: Cover and p. 12 © Finley-Holiday/FPG International Corp.; p. 4 © Telegraph Colour Library; pp. 7, 8, 11, 20 © FPG International Corp.; pp. 12, 15 © Alex Bartel 1990/FPG International Corp.; pp. 16, 17 © Jack Zehrt/FPG International Corp.; p. 19 © NASA 1990.

Davis, Amanda
      Black Holes / by Amanda Davis
            p.   cm. — (Exploring Space)
      Includes index.
      Summary: Briefly describes the formation and composition of black holes and the forces connected with them.
      ISBN 0-8239-5061-1
      1. Black holes (Astronomy)—Juvenile literature. [1. Black holes (Astronomy).]
      I. Title. II. Series: Davis, Amanda. Exploring space.
      QB843.B55D39 1997
      523.8'875—dc21
                                                                                          96–53487
                                                                                              CIP
                                                                                              AC

Manufactured in the United States of America

Contents

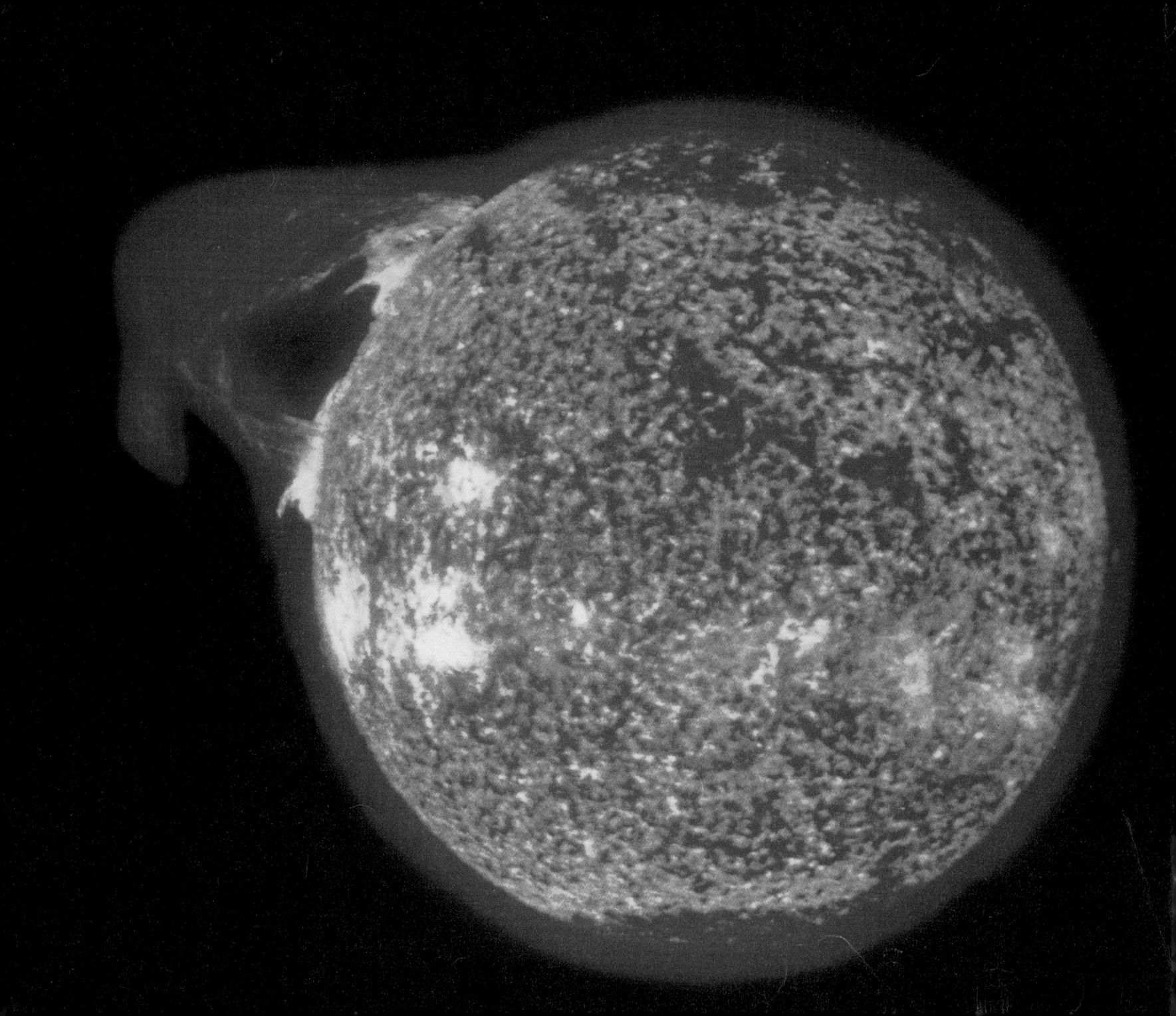

There's No Hole in a Black Hole

Did you know that a black hole is not really a hole at all? It used to be a star. When a very big star dies, it **collapses** (kul-AP-sez) and forms a black hole.

There are many different kinds of stars in the **universe** (YOO-nih-vers). Stars live and die like we do. White dwarves, red giants, supergiants, and black holes are examples of different stages in a star's life.

Some stars last for billions of years, some only for 100 million.

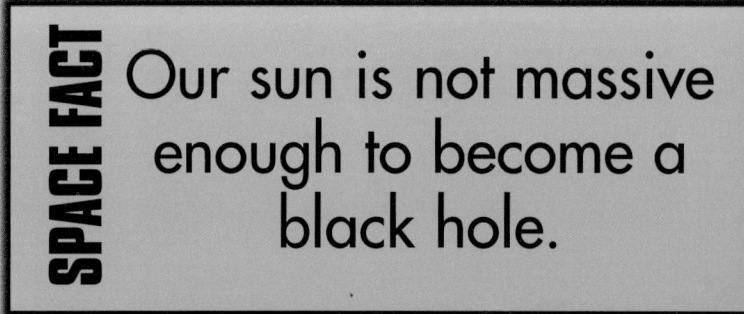

SPACE FACT Our sun is not massive enough to become a black hole.

◀ Our sun is an example of one kind of star. It is called a red giant.

The Life Cycle of a Star

Black holes don't start off as black holes. They begin like all stars do, as a huge gas cloud in space. When the gas cloud collapses in on itself, a star is formed.

Gas from the original cloud becomes the star's **fuel** (FYOOL). Stars burn that fuel throughout their lives. When that fuel runs out, the star dies.

SPACE FACT

A red dwarf is one stage of a star's life. It is one of the coolest stages of the life cycle of a star.

Without gas clouds, there would be no stars or black holes. ▶

Black Holes Are Massive

What happens to a star at the end of its life? That depends on how much **mass** (MASS) the star has.

Mass measures how much stuff something is made of. Size measures how big something is. For example, a blown-up balloon is much larger than a baseball. But the baseball has more mass than the balloon. That's why it weighs more.

Stars with large amounts of mass become black holes. Even though they are very massive, black holes are much smaller than most stars.

◄ A supernova occurs when a very big star explodes. It only happens in some stars and it is very bright.

Right before a star dies it gets hundreds of times brighter than usual.

The Gravity of a Black Hole

A black hole has very strong **gravity** (GRAV-ih-tee).

Gravity is a natural **force** (FORSS) between all objects. This force causes objects to be attracted to each other. Gravity is what causes gas clouds to cave in on themselves and form stars.

The more massive an object is, the stronger its gravity. Black holes are some of the most massive objects in the universe. Because they are so massive, the gravity of a black hole is incredibly strong. Objects and particles that are floating near the black hole are pulled into it because of its strong gravity.

Gravity is what causes moons to orbit their planets, like Jupiter and its moons. ▶

Why Don't Black Holes Shine?

A black hole's gravity is so strong that even light can't escape from it!

Light is actually made up of tiny **particles** (PAR-tih-kulz) and **waves** (WAYVZ). Gravity pulls on light just like it does on baseballs or people. Light travels very fast, at 186,000 miles per second! But light does not travel fast enough to escape a black hole's gravity. The light never escapes from the black hole, so we never see it. That's why a black hole doesn't shine the way a star, like our sun, does.

◀ The particles around a black hole are often in a swirl, or circle.

Black Holes Are Hard to Study

It is hard for scientists to study black holes with the methods they use to study space. Scientists use many kinds of **signals** (SIG-nulz) to study other things in space. The light from stars and light reflected from other objects, such as planets, are signals that provide lots of information for scientists. Other signals such as **radio waves** (RAY-dee-oh WAYVZ) and **X rays** (EKS-RAYZ) help scientists to study space too.

It's hard to study a black hole because none of these signals can escape from the black hole. So scientists have to use other ways to learn about them.

Scientists use special tools, such as this very strong antenna, to receive signals from space. ▶

Can We See Black Holes?

If a star is circling very fast around an object in space that we can't see, that object might be a black hole. The black hole's gravity is what causes the star to **orbit** (OR-bit) around it so fast.

If a star or part of a star falls into a black hole, X rays will shoot out into space just before the star falls in. **Telescopes** (TEL-uh-skohps) let scientists study this burst of X rays. That tells us that a black hole is probably there.

◀ Telescopes are one way people on Earth can study black holes.

How Many Black Holes Are There?

Many stars in the universe are massive enough to become black holes. Stephen Hawking, one of today's great **astronomers** (uh-STRON-uh-merz), believes that there might be more black holes in the universe than stars that we can see.

There may even be an enormous black hole right in the middle of our **galaxy** (GAL-ik-see), which is called the Milky Way. Some believe this black hole may be over 100,000 times as massive as our sun!

SPACE FACT Objects are safe from a black hole until they reach the "event horizon." Once they pass this point, they cannot escape the gravity and will be sucked into the black hole!

Galaxies, like this one, often look like a big swirl of dust. ▶

Will Earth Be Sucked into a Black Hole?

Things in space are very far apart. The force of gravity between two objects is weak when they are far apart. Even though a black hole has very strong gravity, it is not strong enough to pull something into it unless it is very close.

You can think of a black hole as a vacuum cleaner. A vacuum cleaner can't suck something up that is far away. Our planet Earth is not close enough to any black holes to be sucked into one.

SPACE FACT

Four possible black holes have been detected in our galaxy.

◀ Even though pictures make planets look close together, they are really thousands, or even millions, of miles apart.

Time

One of the strangest things about a black hole is that it causes time to change.

Albert Einstein was a famous **scientist** (SY-en-tist) who was born in 1879 and died in 1955. He discovered that time changes in certain situations. A black hole's strong pull of gravity causes things near it to travel very fast. Because of this, time is slower near a black hole than it is on Earth.

We don't know a lot about black holes. But they may help us learn more about gravity and time. Scientists continue to study black holes with the hope that they will learn more about them and about the universe.

Glossary

astronomer (uh-STRON-uh-mer) A person who studies space.

collapse (kul-APS) To fall down or cave in.

force (FORSS) Something in nature that causes action.

fuel (FYOOL) A liquid or a gas that allows something to have power.

galaxy (GAL-ik-see) A system of stars, planets, and other space objects.

gravity (GRAV-ih-tee) A force between two objects that causes them to be attracted to each other.

mass (MASS) The amount of material in something.

orbit (OR-bit) When one thing circles another.

particle (PAR-tih-kul) A tiny piece of matter.

radio wave (RAY-dee-oh WAYV) An invisible ripple in space that can be picked up by certain instruments.

scientist (SY-en-tist) A person who studies the world and the universe.

signal (SIG-nul) A sign giving notice of something.

telescope (TEL-uh-skohp) An instrument that makes the stars and planets easier to see and study.

universe (YOO-nih-vers) Everything that exists. Our solar system is just a small part of the universe.

wave (WAYV) An invisible ripple in space.

X ray (EKS-RAY) One kind of invisible ripple that is used to study space.

Index